Amazing Animals
Giraffes

Please visit our web site at www.garethstevens.com
For a free catalog describing our list of high-quality books, call 1-800-542-2595 (USA) or 1-800-387-3178 (Canada).
Our fax: 1-877-542-2596

Library of Congress Cataloging-in-Publication Data

Albee, Sarah.
    Giraffes / by Sarah Albee.
            p. cm.—(Amazing Animals)
        Originally published: Pleasantville, NY : Reader's Digest Young Familiies, c2006.
        Includes bibliographical references and index.
        ISBN-10: 0-8368-9097-3 (lib. bdg.)   ISBN-13: 978-0-8368-9097-6
    1. Giraffe—Juvenile literature. I. Title.
    QL737.U56A43 2009
    599.638—dc22   2008013373

This edition first published in 2009 by
Gareth Stevens Publishing
A Weekly Reader® Company
1 Reader's Digest Road
Pleasantville, NY 10570-7000 USA

Gareth Stevens Senior Managing Editor: Lisa M. Herrington
Gareth Stevens Creative Director: Lisa Donovan
Gareth Stevens Art Director: Ken Crossland
Gareth Stevens Associate Editor: Amanda Hudson

Consultant: Robert E. Budliger (Retired), NY State Department of Environmental Conservation

Photo Credits
Front cover: PhotoDisc by Getty Images. Title page: Brand X Pictures. Contents page: IT Stock. page 6-7: IT Stock. page 8 (upper left): Nova
Development Corporation. page 8-9: Digital Vision. page 10 (lower left): Brand X Pictures. page 10-11 Digital Vision. page 12-13: Brand X
Pictures. page 13 (lower right): Nova Development Corporation. page 14-15: Digital Vision. page 16-17: Digital Vision. page 18-19: Corbis
Corporation. page 19 (lower right): John Foxx Images. page 20 (upper left): Nova Development Corporation. page 22-23: Dynamic Graphics, Inc.
page 23 (lower right): Nova Development Corporation. page 24-25: Digital Vision. page 26-27: Dynamic Graphics. page 28-29: Digital Vision.
page 30-31: Corbis Corporation. page 32-33: PhotoDisc, Inc. page 34-35: Image 100 ltd. page 38-39: PhotoDisc, Inc. page 42-43: Dynamic
Graphics, Inc. page 44-45: PhotoDisc, Inc. page 46: John Foxx Images. Back cover: Digital Vision.

Every effort has been made to trace the copyright holders for the photos used in this book, and the publisher apologizes in advance for any unin-
tentional omissions. We would be pleased to insert the appropriate acknowledgements in any subsequent edition of this publication.

Printed in the United States of America

1 2 3 4 5 6 7 8 9 10 09

Amazing Animals
Giraffes

By Sarah Albee

Gareth Stevens
Publishing
A WEEKLY READER COMPANY

Contents

Chapter 1
A Giraffe Story

Day Care

For the first four or five months of their lives, baby giraffes rest and play in small groups called crèches. Their mothers search for food.

The sun is shining across the African **savanna**. The rainy season has finally ended. A giraffe is ready to have her baby. With a thud, a bundle falls to the ground. A baby giraffe is born. The newborn **calf** is unhurt, and her mother nuzzles her lovingly.

About twenty minutes later, the baby staggers to her feet. She is already 6 feet (1.8 meters) tall! Two little horns lie flat against her head, but they'll pop up in a week or so. For two weeks, the mother giraffe hides her baby in the tall grass to keep her safe.

At first, the baby giraffe spends most of the time lying down. As her legs grow stronger, she begins to walk more and more. When she is hungry, she cries for her mother, who is never far away.

Several months go by, and the baby grows quickly. She still drinks milk from her mother, but now she joins the group of other giraffes as they look for leaves from **acacia** trees.

One day, while the mother is guarding the babies, she sounds an alarm. With snorts and hisses, she alerts the other adults grazing nearby to come quickly. She has spotted a female lion creeping toward the group of young giraffes. The other mothers run back to the group. The young giraffe races to her mother, who positions herself above her baby to protect her.

The lion stops. She knows that one kick from the mother giraffe's front legs could be deadly. The lion gives up the hunt and trots away.

Giant Giraffes

The ancestors of giraffes that lived around 25 million years ago may have been even taller than giraffes are today.

A Good Defense

Some scientists believe that other kinds of animals, like zebras and antelopes, intentionally graze near groups of giraffes. The giraffes' ability to spot danger from a distance helps protect these other animals, too.

Excuse Me!

Giraffes burp a lot. It's the way they release the gaseous wastes from all the leaves they eat!

After five years, the giraffe is fully grown. She walks with a group of other giraffes, munching leaves. She knows her friends and relatives by the markings on their coats. An oxpecker bird perches on her back and plucks insects from her coat.

The giraffe will soon be ready to have a calf of her own. She will stay in the same area where her mother lives for the rest of her life.

It's a Stretch

Male and female giraffes eat leaves that grow at different heights. Males reach up to leaves growing higher than they are, with their heads and necks stretched upward. Females eat at the level of their body, sometimes with their head and neck slightly bent.

Chapter 2
The Body of a Giraffe

Neck and Neck

You have seven bones in your neck. So does a giraffe! The difference is that the giraffe's bones are much longer than yours.

The neck of a fully-grown giraffe is taller than most adult humans!

Tall and Towering

Giraffes are the tallest animals in the world. They do not have to compete with other animals for food because they can reach food that other animals cannot. Their height also allows them to spot **predators** from far away.

Giraffes have a brown **mane** along their necks. Their manes are short and bristly. Giraffes have long tails with a tuft of stiff hair at the ends—perfect for swatting away insects.

Giraffes may look alike to us, but their coats vary. The background color ranges from white to tan to yellowish. Giraffes' spots can be anywhere from light orange to dark brown. The shape of the spots also differ. The pattern on a giraffe's coat stays the same throughout its life, but the color darkens as the giraffe gets older.

Spot the Difference

The markings on a giraffe's coat are different on each animal. No two are exactly alike! This helps giraffes recognize one another.

Can Giraffes Jump?

Giraffes are able to jump over objects as high as 6 feet (1.8 meters)! That's about as high as a tall man!

A giraffe's front legs are longer than the back ones, giving the giraffe a slightly downward slope.

Long Legs

With its long legs, a giraffe can cover a lot of ground, even when it is just walking. You would have to run to keep up!

A giraffe has two strides—walking and galloping. When walking, the giraffe swings both right legs forward at the same time and then both left legs. Only one other animal walks this way—the camel! Other animals with four legs, such as dogs, walk by moving diagonally opposite legs—the front right and back left legs and then the front left and back right ones.

As it gallops, the giraffe swings its great neck backward and forward like a huge rocking horse. At a gallop, a giraffe moves 10 feet (3 m) with each stride, thundering along at more than 30 miles (48 kilometers) per hour! Most of the time, though, giraffes stroll slowly, munching leaves as they go.

Horn of Plenty

All giraffes are born with two horns on top of their heads. Some male giraffes have as many as five! As the giraffe gets older, its horns grow harder and stiffer.

Sight and Smell

With their height and excellent eyesight, giraffes can see far across the flat African plains. Their huge eyes are protected by long lashes and are set on the sides of their heads so that the animal can see all around. Some animals feel safer near giraffes because they can detect predators when they are far away.

Giraffes also have a good sense of smell. A mother giraffe recognizes her baby by the way it smells. Giraffe scent glands give off an odor that helps them to recognize one another. Their odor probably also protects them from pesky insects.

Do Giraffes Make Sounds?

Many people think that giraffes are silent animals, but they are not! They tend to be quiet, but giraffes can make many sounds, such as moans, alarm calls, snorts, and hisses. Baby giraffes cry. Mother giraffes, calling to their babies, may even bellow!

Giraffes have great hearing.
Their long ears can swivel in
several directions!

A Dozing Pose

Giraffes sometimes sleep sitting down with their legs folded beneath them, but with their neck held upright.

Giraffes sometimes nap while standing up.

Catching a Few Winks

Giraffes rest after dark in an open area where they can keep an eye out for danger. They lie down for a few hours to rest and chew their **cud,** catching bits of sleep here and there. Giraffes usually sleep deeply for only 1 to 12 minutes at a time and for a total of only about 20 minutes a night. They may keep one eye open to be on the alert for predators. When they do lie down and sleep, they bend their neck backward to rest on their back leg.

Keeping Clean

Giraffes **groom** themselves by biting and licking. Having a very long neck and tongue is helpful for reaching most parts of a giraffe's body!

Giraffes also have cleaning helpers—birds that live with them. The buffalo weaver and birds perch on the giraffes and pluck out biting insects from their fur. The birds also help by calling when they spot danger.

Chapter 3
Lunch Munchers

Far Reaching

A giraffe's tongue is 18 inches (46 centimeters) long! A giraffe uses its tongue to grasp leaves that are out of its reach and to clean its eyes and ears.

Giraffes spend half of each day eating.

Plant Eaters

Giraffes are **herbivores**. They eat only plants. The leaves of the acacia tree are their favorite. Most acacia trees have long, sharp thorns. But these don't bother the giraffes. With their strong lips and long tongues, the giraffes gather the leaves into their mouths and tear them off the branches by pulling their heads away.

Luckily for acacia trees, giraffes do not eat all the leaves on a tree before moving on. One reason may be the stinging ants that live in hollow areas of the branches. The giraffes will only put up with the stings for a short time. Then they move on.

Chewing Their Cud

Just like cows, giraffes belong to a type of animal called **ruminants**. Ruminants have a stomach with four compartments that help break down the tough leaves that the animals eat.

When giraffes are not eating, they are chewing their cud. The cud is a ball of partly digested leaves that travels back up their throat into their mouths for further grinding.

A Tall Drink of Water

Drinking water is a difficult task for the world's tallest animals. It is hard for them to reach the level of the water.

A giraffe's front legs are so long that the giraffe must spread them to the sides in order to lower its head to the water. This is an awkward position. Sometimes giraffes kneel down to drink, but this position is hard to get in and out of, too.

Have you ever bent your head down very low and then straightened up quickly? If so, you may have felt dizzy. Imagine, then, how a giraffe feels when it lowers its head 18 feet (5 m)! Fortunately, a giraffe has a special system to manage this problem. Inside the giraffe's neck are **blood vessels** that stretch. Inside the blood vessels are **valves** (like little trap doors) that prevent all the blood from rushing to the animal's head as it dips way below its heart. Without these valves, the giraffe could faint every time it drinks because of the changes in its blood pressure.

After a giraffe stands up, it usually stretches its neck and back legs to get the blood flowing freely again.

Dry Spells

Like camels, giraffes can go for weeks without drinking any water. They get most of the moisture they need from the leaves they eat.

When a giraffe's legs are splayed, the giraffe is vulnerable to attack. It can't quickly stand up to flee or defend itself.

Chapter 4
Surviving in the Wild

A mother giraffe usually returns to the same place every time she has a baby.

Young Giraffes

After carrying the baby inside her body for about 14 months, a mother giraffe gives birth standing up, usually to a single calf.

A giraffe is huge from the moment it is born. A newborn calf is 6 feet (1.8 m) tall and 150 pounds (68 kg)—the size of a grown man!

Young calves are playful and love to run around together. For the first four to five months of their lives, the calves stay together in a small group called a crèche. They play or rest while their mothers search for food. At least one adult female stays with the calves for protection. Young giraffes are most often attacked by predators during their first year of life. Once they are a year old, though, they have a very good chance of living to 20 to 25 years of age.

Giraffe Herds

Giraffes live in loose, open groups called herds. A herd may spread across half a mile of the savanna.

A giraffe herd may consist of mothers and their young, or be all males, or be a mix of males and females. The members of giraffe herds are always changing. The herds usually don't have a leader.

Most herds have up to 20 giraffes. Because of their large size, giraffes do not need to live closely together for safety. With their height and sharp eyesight, they can warn each other of any danger.

The home ranges of giraffes can vary greatly, but average about as big as a medium-sized city. Males eventually leave their home range to mate, but females tend to stay close to the area where they were born for life.

Living in small groups helps giraffes protect themselves and their young.

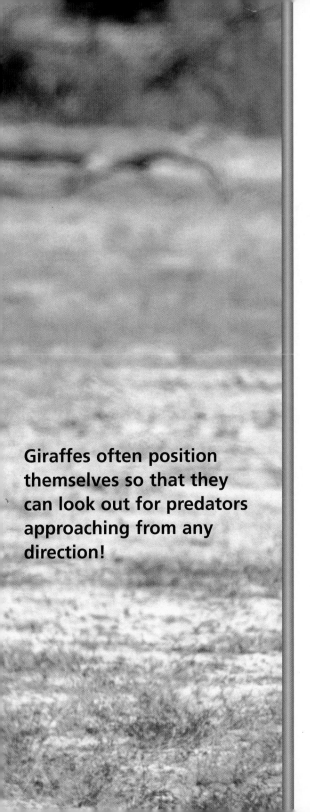

Giraffes often position themselves so that they can look out for predators approaching from any direction!

Protecting Themselves

Adult giraffes have few enemies. That's because they are so big and because the markings on their coat help them blend in with their surroundings.

The only predators that adult giraffes fear, besides humans, are lions and crocodiles. Adult giraffes are most in danger when they bend down to drink or lie down to sleep. Fortunately for giraffes, they don't need to drink very often, and they sleep for only a few minutes at a time.

Young giraffes, though, are often **preyed** upon by lions, leopards, hyenas, and wild dogs. Mother giraffes protect their calves by kicking attackers with their strong front legs, which can kill a full-grown lion.

Chapter 5
Giraffes in the World

Leaf Spots

Giraffes with dark brown, leaf-shaped spots on a yellowish background are called Masai giraffes.

Giraffes with large patches that are clearly outlined are called reticulated giraffes.

Spot the Spots

Although each giraffe has its own special color and spot pattern on its coat, scientists have identified and named about eight groups of giraffes that have similar patterns and share the same home range.

Some groups of giraffes have large spots. Others have small ones. Certain giraffes have round spots. Others have spots with sides. Spots can also be star-shaped, leaf-shaped, or no regular shape!

Only Relative

The giraffe has only one close relative, the okapi. Although the okapi has a dark coat (with no patches) and stripes on its legs, it has an elongated neck. The okapi lives in the African rain forests.

41

Where Giraffes Live

Twenty-five million years ago, giraffes lived in what is now Africa, Europe, and Asia. Today's giraffes are found only in Africa, south of the Sahara Desert. Giraffes live on the savanna and in open woodlands, most often where acacia trees grow. Once hunted by humans for food, their hides, and tail hair, giraffes are now protected by laws in many countries.

Fast Facts About Giraffes

Scientific name	*Giraffa camelopardalis*
Class	Mammals
Family	*Giraffidae*
Size	Males 18 feet (5.5 m) tall
	Females 16 feet (4.9 m) tall
Weight	Males up to 3,000 pounds (1,360 kg)
	Females up to 1,500 pounds (680 kg)
Habitat	Savannas and open woodlands with tall trees
Speed	Up to 30 miles (48 km) per hour

A Giraffe Is Not a Camel!

Despite its scientific name, *Giraffa camelopardalis*, the giraffe is not related to the camel. When giraffes were first brought to Rome, they were believed to be a type of camel that was spotted like a leopard. Today we know that giraffes are a unique **species**.

The word *giraffe* comes from an Arabic word meaning "one who walks swiftly."

Glossary of Wild Words

acacia — a tree that grows in warm areas and has feather-like leaves

blood vessels — the arteries and veins in a body through which blood flows to and from the heart

calf — a baby or young giraffe

cud — food that comes back into an animal's mouth from the stomach for the animal to chew again

groom — to clean fur, skin, or feathers by an animal

habitat — the natural environment where an animal or plant lives

herbivore — an animal that eats only plants

mammal — an animal with a backbone and hair on its body that drinks milk from its mother when it is born

mane — hair on the head or neck of an animal

predator — an animal that hunts and eats other animals to survive

prey — animals that are hunted by other animals for food

ruminants — hoofed mammals that have four chambers in their stomachs and that chew cud

savanna — a flat grassland area with scattered trees in a hot region of the world

species — a group of plants or animals that are the same in many ways

splay — to spread outward in an awkward way

swivel — to twist or turn around on the same spot

valve — a device that starts or stops the flow of liquid

Giraffes: Show What You Know

How much have you learned about giraffes? Grab a piece of paper and a pencil and write your answers down.

1. What is the name of the small group that baby giraffes rest and play in?

2. How do giraffes release gaseous wastes from the leaves they eat?

3. How many bones does a giraffe have in its neck?

4. Why is a giraffe vulnerable when it drinks water?

5. How do mother giraffes defend their babies if they are attacked?

6. Which animal is the only close relative of giraffes?

7. How does a giraffe's coat change as it gets older?

8. What three predators do adult giraffes fear?

9. On what continent are giraffes found today?

10. How fast can giraffes run?

1. Crèche 2. They burp 3. 7 4. Because it can't stand up quickly to defend itself 5. By kicking with their front legs 6. The okapi 7. The color gets darker 8. Humans, lions, and crocodiles 9. Africa 10. Up to 30 miles (48 kilometers) per hour

For More Information

Books

Giraffe: Habitats, Life Cycles, Food Chains, Threats. Natural World (series). Leach, Michael (Steck-Vaughn, 2001)

Giraffes. All About Wild Animals (series). (Gareth Stevens, 2005)

Web Sites

African Savanna: Giraffe

http://nationalzoo.si.edu/Animals/AfricanSavanna/fact-giraffe.cfm

The National Zoo features giraffes and interesting facts about them. Find out why the ancient Romans called these animals "camelopards."

Giraffe Central: Zoo Fact Sheets

http://www.isidore-of-seville.com/giraffe/2.html

From this site, you can link to pages about giraffes that have been posted by many zoos. See what zookeepers at the San Diego Zoo and elsewhere have to say.

Publisher's note to educators and parents: Our editors have carefully reviewed these web sites to ensure that they are suitable for children. Many web sites change frequently, however, and we cannot guarantee that a site's future contents will continue to meet our high standards of quality and educational value. Be advised that children should be closely supervised whenever they access the Internet.

Index